Frank Lloyd Wright's
PUBLIC BUILDINGS

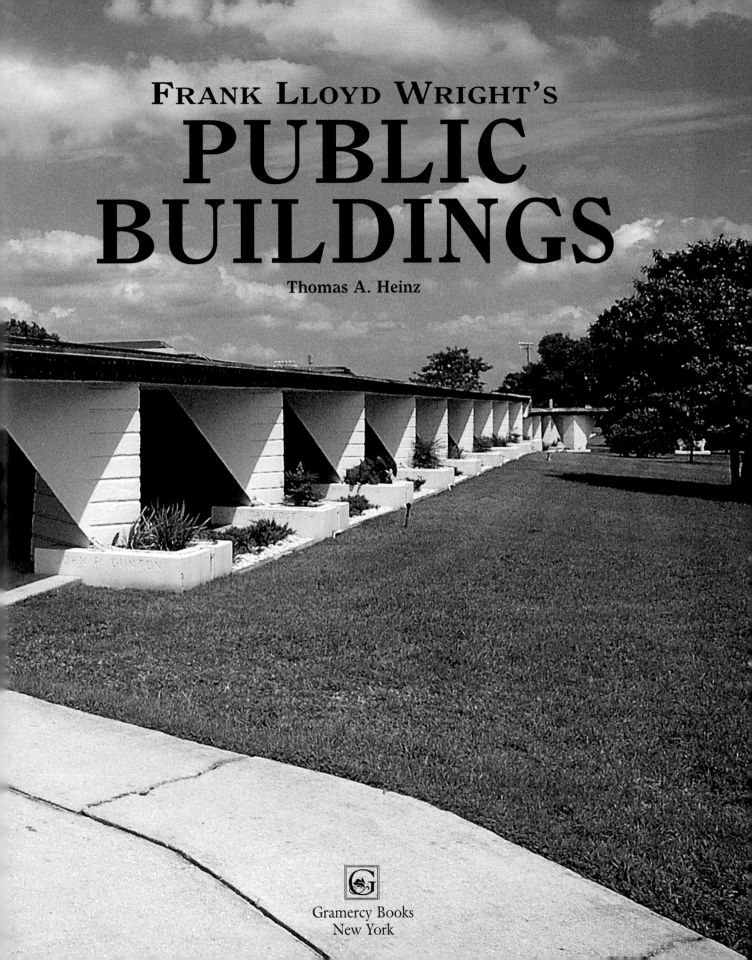

Frank Lloyd Wright's
PUBLIC BUILDINGS

Thomas A. Heinz

Gramercy Books
New York

This 2002 edition is published by
Gramercy Books™, an imprint of
Random House Value Publishing, Inc.,
280 Park Avenue, New York, NY 10017

Gramercy Books™ and design are
trademarks of Random House Value
Publishing, Inc.

Random House
New York • Toronto • London
Sydney • Auckland

http://www.randomhouse.com/

Printed in Italy

ISBN 0-517-21970-0

10 9 8 7 6 5 4 3 2 1

*Dedicated to Olgivanna Lloyd Wright
who, more than anyone else, brought
Frank Lloyd Wright's buildings to the
public attention.*

It is essential that a workable system
of preservation and restoration be
coordinated between the existing
owners of the many remaining
examples of Frank Lloyd Wright's
buildings for, unless they are
maintained in their original colours,
materials and arrangements, how can
anyone make a proper assessment of
their worth, even to the point of
whether they like them or not. An
assessment cannot be made based on
photographs, or on memories of
buildings that no longer reflect the
work as Wright conceived and
approved it and personally directed its
execution. Wright's work is too
important to allow further deterioration
and demolition and readers must try to
participate in this effort of preservation,
even if it is only to involve others in
the appreciation of Wright's work.

The end of the 19th century was a period that saw new materials and technologies being steadily developed. This included cast and reinforced concrete, which in conjunction with steel frames and larger glass panels was allowing more innovative building solutions than had up till then been possible. It was the beginning of the era of the skyscraper.

From 1888–1893, Frank Lloyd Wright worked as a draftsman in the company of Dankmar Adler and Louis H. Sullivan, a partnership very much in the vanguard of architectural development in America, and which specialized in commercial buildings. It is surprising, therefore, that in his long career Wright did not receive more commissions of this type, when one thinks how he must have benefited from Adler's engineering expertise, not to mention the influence of Sullivan, that great proponent of American Art

UNITY CHAPEL, SPRING GREEN, WISCONSIN, 1886

Designed by Joseph Lyman Silsbee, after he had arrived in Chicago from Syracuse and had become acquainted with the Rev. Jenkin Lloyd Jones, Frank Lloyd Wright's uncle, the chapel was constructed by the Rev. Jones' brother, Thomas Lloyd Jones. There is evidence that a 'boy architect' gave some assistance with the project and, though the boy was not named, it has always been assumed that it was the young Frank Lloyd Wright, the only member of the family that seems to fit the bill.

ROMEO & JULIET WINDMILL, SPRING GREEN, WISCONSIN, 1896

Frank's uncles, who up till then had designed and constructed most of the buildings in the Jones Valley, were not very impressed with their nephew's design of a windmill which had been asked for by his aunts. The tower has a bamboo-like appearance, while each of the corners of the structure have continuous wooden members which take both the compression to leeward and the tension on the windward side, providing good balance from side to side. These vertical wooden members were bolted to metal straps that were anchored into the deep stone foundation. The windmill brought water to a reservoir and then through pipes for inside running water for the school buildings just a little way down the hill.

Nouveau for whom, in fact, Wright had the greater reverence.

Moreover, Wright's 1904 design for the Larkin company of Buffalo, New York was one of the most outstanding examples of an office building, with many revolutionary features remarkable in this the first of Wright's large-scale projects. Why then were there not more Larkin types built?

This is a difficult question to answer, as Wright appears to have received the Larkin commission largely through his work and contacts at a residential level. He had designed many houses, including some for Larkin executives, and this seems to have been the primary reason for their choice, rather than Wright's previous commercial experience.

However, Wright contrived to improve his public image by

designing his first skyscraper, the San Francisco Press Building in 1912, just before the sale of the newspaper to William Randolph Hearst. That elegantly tall building, however, was never built.

Of all the unbuilt designs that Wright left us after his death, the National Life Insurance Building of 1924 is the one that would have changed the direction of his career. It had all the elements that would have made it one of the world's great buildings, while the site was one of the best in any American city, where it would have been seen as a landmark on a wide boulevard facing south at a bend in the road. The building itself was to have been of glass and copper, forming a 24-storey jewel-like structure. The floor plan formed an efficient arrangement with plenty of elevators to speed the occupants in

FRANK LLOYD WRIGHT STUDIO, OAK PARK, ILLINOIS, 1897

ABOVE: Plaque attached to the wall of the studio.

ABOVE: The entry to the studio.

and out. If there are any doubts as to its viability, a look at the magnificent drawings will remove such uncertainties.

The client, Albert M. Johnson, was wealthy, enthusiastic and a great salesman, who employed men of similar talent, including the

FRANK LLOYD WRIGHT STUDIO, OAK PARK, ILLINOIS, 1897

Henry Hobson Richardson, the most influential figure in mid-19th century American architecture, regarded his work as the most important thing in his life, and integrated his office into his household in much the same way that Wright did when he added the studio wing to his 1889 home.

Wright expressed the building's interior functions using the elements shown here. On the right is an octagonal library which was also used as a private conference room where discussions with clients took place. To the left of that is the entry and reception area where guests were greeted and where prospective contractors arrived to present their bids. Behind the entry wasWright's office with its own skylight and view of the front garden.

The two-storey square structure on the left with the octagonal drum above it was the drafting room where blueprints were produced. This room had no columns, even though there was a suspended balcony on all sides. The balcony was held in place by a chain harness that connected to the roof and walls. The open first level allowed different arrangements of the drafting tables, depending on the work in hand.

The photograph shows the studio in the form that Wright left it in about 1911, after remodelling it into two apartments that were intended to provide an income for his family, after he had abandoned them and moved into Taliesin with Mamah Borthwick Cheney.

MacArthurs of Oak Park who became more wealthy than Johnson himself (the John D. MacArthur Foundation still supports the arts). A brother, Charles, wrote *Front Page*, and all the brothers owned a publishing company that included the local newspaper, *Oak Leaves*.

Albert Johnson had already been a client when Wright's search for adventure took him to Death Valley in California and where Wright had designed an unusual desert compound for him in 1922.

By the late 1930s, Wright's celebrity had considerably increased due to the construction of the Johnson Wax Building and Edgar Kaufmann's house, Fallingwater – so much so that in 1938 Wright, together with an image of Fallingwater, was featured on the cover of *Time* magazine, signalling to the commercial world that Wright had crossed the line between artist/rebel and public figure/man of genius; this valuable publicity in a respected journal exposed Wright to a greater number of potential clients than he might otherwise have reached by more conventional means. In fact, about half of these larger commissions came Wright's way during the last period of his working life, the Usonian period.

HILLSIDE HOME SCHOOL, SPRING GREEN, WISCONSIN, 1897 (ABOVE)
Shown after additions and conversion by Wright to include facilities for the Taliesin Fellowship in 1932 and after.

LARKIN COMPANY ADMINISTRATION BUILDING, BUFFALO, NEW YORK, 1904 (OPPOSITE ABOVE)
One of the first of Wright's large-scale commercial enterprises, it is a tragedy that this innovative building was later destroyed.

The entry could possibly have been located in the centre of the broad base of the main office block, but in fact it was not, but was up a

broad set of stairs, past a fountain and pool, through a set of sturdy doors, where a semi-circular desk was set at nearly the centre of the building at the point where the low annexe meets with the taller office block. The red brick was trimmed with nearly matching sandstone. The big brick shoulders housed the stairs and air shafts that delivered and removed conditioned and stale air.

Although the Larkin building was only five storeys high, it appears to be a much larger structure because of the lack of the common scalar elements. The bricks are rather larger than normal and the windows are set deep into the walls.

Taken as a whole over Wright's 70-year career, however, these larger public buildings appear to have no style or theme in common. In fact, there are great variations in size and scale, from what may be the smallest, the 1886 Jones family's Unity Chapel, in Spring Green, Wisconsin, from the beginning of his career, to by far the largest, the 1957 Marin County Civic Center.

As its name suggests, one of the largest conceived was the Mile High building for Chicago. The design, however, was never realized but still manages to stir the imagination of architects and manufacturers of building products

and systems. It was designed around the same time as the Marin County Civic Center.

Wright's public buildings have a timeless quality about them: Marin County was recently used in a movie – 50 years after its completion – as a building set in the far future, as have many of Wright's other designs, while the Ennis house provided a backdrop for *Blade Runner* as well as *Supergirl*, also set in the future. This is all the more remarkable as Wright used traditional materials and geometries but still managed to produce buildings which could belong to any age.

Did Wright insist on always having his own way or were there the inevitable compromises? Was Wright anti-corporate? Most of the companies for which he was to design buildings were run by powerful, autocratic men, rather than by committees or bureaucracies. John Larkin, Herbert Johnson, Harold Price and Edgar Kaufmann were all strong individualists, able to make their own decisions and stick by them. Typically, they were clients who were able to see their projects through to the end and, with a degree of give and take with respect to the architect, be satisfied with the final result.

When it came to places of worship Wright did not design exclusively for one religious group, even though there were three Unitarian projects. The others included a Roman Catholic church (for California), one for a Greek Orthodox community, and a Jewish

synagogue. Wright had been raised in a Unitarian family and, on a personal level, was well acquainted with the concerns and perspectives of pastors planning new buildings for their congregations. He understood how difficult it was for radical designs to be accepted. He also knew how obstructive building committees could be and was able to offer advice and make the process run more smoothly.

While it is recognized that Wright was willing to design anything, there are no federal or state buildings in his oeuvre. This is probably as much the result of his revolutionary ideas as his

unconventional personal life.

When Wright left Adler & Sullivan's and decided to go it alone, he had been renting office space in the central business district of Chicago for several years but still needed a place to work outside office hours when inspiration called. By 1897, with his growing family also requiring space, his 1889 Oak Park house needed to be expanded again, as it was in 1895 when a new kitchen and children's playroom was added.

The solution was to use the large area adjacent to the house to build a studio where he could work and that would allow him more

time to take meals with his family as well as reduce the time taken to commute to an office. Moreover, many of his prospective clients lived in and around Oak Park and would be able to consult him locally. Wright also welcomed the prospect of a project of his own, rather than having to cater to a client's personal needs.

Wright was responsible for the design of several impressive corporate headquarters, which brought a certain notoriety because of the unconventional methods he used when resolving particular difficulties. The first was the Larkin Company Building of 1904 and the

THE ROOKERY BUILDING, CHICAGO, ILLINOIS, 1905 (OPPOSITE AND ABOVE) *Wright was responsible for the remodelling of the entrances and the court staircase and balcony of the original Burnham & Root Rookery Building. The detailing appears to be a throwback to the pre-1900 era, as does the elaborate gold leaf used throughout which may have been at the request of the client, Edward C. Waller. The glass-covered court, besides letting in light, important before the era of electricity, had allowed the original architects to include the spectacular staircase on the west wall, which pierces the glass-ceilinged lobby.*

problem was its location in a dense, much-polluted industrial area, where a clean environment was preferable for processing the orders the company received by mail. Conditioned air was thus required, and Wright designed a system that cleaned the air as well as humidified it and in summer cooled it as well. It was necessary to seal the windows to keep the interior clean, and supplementary lighting was needed in the form of skylights so that the floor widths could be fixed at about 30ft (10m).

Nikola Tesla's power station for Westinghouse and the Niagara Falls Power Company near Buffalo was

completed in 1905, round about the same time as the Larkin building, and the abundance of cheap electricity helped to make the Larkin manufacturing plants rather more efficient. Tesla was the first to develop the alternating current induction motor, a necessity of modern life as we know it today.

According to Jack Quinan, an expert on much of Wright's Buffalo work, John Larkin would much rather have hired Wright's mentor, Louis Sullivan, who was unfortunately no longer in the business of designing tall buildings following the death of his partner, Dankmar Adler. In fact, all the

UNITY TEMPLE, OAK PARK, ILLINOIS, 1906

As with the earlier Larkin and later Johnson Wax buildings, the entry to this imposing landmark is at the centre of the building behind the wall and between the large concrete blocks. Three of the sides of the temple room are identical, as are those of the social room. All the columns are identical, and were made by pouring concrete into the same re-usable moulds, which made for an economical building. Inexpensive concrete was also used elsewhere as stone, or even brick would have more than doubled the initial construction cost and the building would possibly have deteriorated more quickly. Again, by eliminating scalar elements such as brick, the façade is much more imposing than its small scale would lead one to expect; the building also uses oversized elements to obscure the scale further. The base where the wall meets the ground is over 4ft (1.2m) tall.

executives of the Larkin company were from Chicago and were familiar with the latest trends in building in that city.

Wright appears to have come to the project through a contractor who had been responsible for the construction of the J.J. Walser House of 1903. Meanwhile, Larkin boss, Darwin D. Martin and his brother, William, had also became clients for whom Wright built houses.

Buffalo was an important centre of transportation, in much the same way that Chicago was later to

UNITY TEMPLE, OAK PARK, ILLINOIS, 1906

Unity Temple is one of the finest examples of a building where a full integration of all the systems has gone into the making of the whole. The structure is both expressed and concealed. The roof is also the ceiling of the temple room, shown here, and is a pierced waffle construction with deep beams defining the skylights. The walls are flat on the outside but have a triangular cantilever on the inside that holds the first and second balconies and are tied to the internal hollow columns by deep beams which span them. Inside the columns at each corner of the main floor are air ducts, used to heat the space.

The high clerestory windows not only allow light to filter down to the balconies and the main floor, but the walls below also eliminate most of the noise from the busy street just outside. Skylights with coloured glass give a golden ambience as if the sun were perpetually shining. Hanging lights, two at each pier, tie the roof to the space below with the double globes parted by light cubes.

become. Before Nikola Tesla's development of alternating current in Buffalo, direct current could only be distributed for a few miles, and Tesla's invention made it possible to extend this for many more. This important development was partly the reason why Wright invented his own system of air conditioning, which was technically as advanced as that of the now-famous Willis Carrier method but not as widely known.

Wright also designed metal office furniture and file cabinets, one of the first instances where

UNITY TEMPLE, OAK PARK, ILLINOIS, 1906

LEFT: Looking up at the temple ceiling.

BELOW: The entrance to the space between the temple room on the left and the social room on the right.

floors, there being no obstacles around which to manoeuver.

There was a wide range of amenities for the employees, including a lounge and a fully-furnished library, and a fifth-floor kitchen and restaurant fitted with Wright-designed furniture where lectures on a wide range of subjects were also offered. Evangelist Billy Sunday once gave an address in the main lightcourt that was a standing room-only event.

Throughout the building were

metal was used in this context. Chairs for secretaries were attached to desks at leg and back, and could be folded down and pushed into the kneehole apertures.

These innovations extended to less glamorous but equally important areas of the building in which Wright devised wall-hung lavatories. Partitions and doors were also hung, but from the ceilings. The reasoning behind these innovations was to make offices and their equipment more effective and easier to clean. Chairs did not have to be put upside-down on the desks and a wide sweep of a mop was all that was required when cleaning lavatory

PETTIT MEMORIAL CHAPEL, BELVIDERE, ILLINOIS, 1906

Dr. W.H. Pettit's brother-in-law was William A Glasner, whose own house, by a ravine in Glencoe, was just about finished when Pettit died in 1905. His wife decided to commission Wright, not only for a memorial headstone, but also for something that would be of benefit to the entire local community for many years to come. The result was a simple chapel, built in the Belvidere cemetery on the Pettit family plot.

scattered slogans and aphorisms, presumably to inspire the employees. At the entry fountain and pool was written: 'Honest Labour needs no Master – Simple Justice needs no Slaves'. Others were from wide-ranging sources, from the Bible and Emerson to a former Larkin employee and founder of the Roycrofters, a social reform community. Others, perhaps, came not only from the founder, John D. Larkin, but also from Frank Lloyd Wright.

Over 1,800 people were employed in the building at one time, working in close proximity with one another with few private offices. Even the general manager, Darwin D. Martin, sat between two others, his desk overlooking the entire first floor where he was able to see all of the other floors.

Internally, the core of the building was an open space, lit from above like an atrium and with tiered galleries on either side, though the five-story building must have seemed quite austere at this

point in time, the Victorian era having ended in 1901. However, the overall structure was immensely powerful with the large square shoulders of brick surrounding the stairs at each corner. The building stood in sharp contrast to the drab buildings of the surrounding neighbourhood.

Sadly, the building was demolished in 1950 and was replaced by a parking lot after it had stood there for over 40 years.

Joseph M. Siry has written a wonderful book which gives the full story of the Unity Temple of 1906 and the conceptual and religious ideas behind its design, its precedents and its troubled existence since its construction nearly 100 years ago. This was not Wright's first religious building; he had been involved with the Unitarian chapel for his uncle Jenkin Lloyd Jones in the family compound at Hillside, just south of Spring Green in the Jones Valley (previously the Helena Valley).

This early chapel, dating from 1886, probably Wright's first venture into the world of architecture, was a three-roomed building, the interior space divided into an auditorium and parlour in typical Victorian fashion. Spanning the ridge of the roof was a small cupola; the exterior of the building had a rather tall stone foundation base, the band formed by the exterior walls filling the span between the stone base and the simple hipped roof. The interior was simpler than the exterior, with plastered walls and a small set of windows grouped together; the ceiling also formed

TALIESIN I, SPRING GREEN, WISCONSIN, 1911 TOWER (LEFT)

This was Taliesin as it was originally, built on land in the Jones Valley which Wright had purchased from his family. Then, it was quite small, but it was replaced on a larger scale after 1914 following damage by fire. It had another reincarnation in 1925.

Opposite the bedroom wing and across from the courtyard and the tea circle is the tower. Over many years and throughout many changes it has held not only the water reservoir, the dinner and alarm bell, but also the accommodation for the chief draftsman, Jack Howe.

ENTRY STAIRS (ABOVE)

The roof connects the little kitchen and the living room of Taliesin with the drafting room. The stairs lead up to the courtyard that is protected by the three wings of Taliesin and is the centre of the complex. The effect or impression of this area is ethereal and seeme to change with the seasons as well as throughout the day.

This is one of the most pleasant ambiences ever created by Wright, who envisaged Taliesin as something more than a house – more as a Welsh medieval manor – with spaces for work and accommodation for Wright's family and apprentices.

the underside of the shingled roof.

Wright's role in the project has not been precisely defined, but he is thought to have been the 'boy architect' referred to in a short article written by the Rev. Jones. The actual architect-in-charge was Joseph Lyman Silsbee, formerly of Rochester, New York who at the time of the construction had moved to Chicago.

Silsbee had recently completed the design and construction of a parish church for the Rev. Jones on Oakwood in a residential neighbourhood just south of Chicago's main business district, the Loop. Both of these buildings were built in the mid-1880s at about the

MIDWAY GARDENS, CHICAGO, ILLINOIS, 1914

Edward C. Waller, Jr. envisaged a grand entertainments complex in the heart of Chicago which was unfortunately ruined by Prohibition and lasted barely ten years.

The Winter Garden (left) was as spatially complex as the exterior, where abstract human forms usually had lighting integrated into them. In the centre was the dance floor, while at the upper right were examples of the few art-glass windows of the second decade of the 1900s. The glass was mostly of a

rather opaque red, white and black.

The number and complexity of textures and ornamental effects added considerably to the gaiety of Midway Gardens. Concrete blocks were used extensively, forerunners of the California block houses of the 1920s, and lighting ran up along nearly every vertical element and under most of the deep overhangs of the roofs. It is said that next to the tallest tower was the architect's box, while tables and chairs were set out to accommodate the vast numbers of customers in the open-air court (above).

time that Wright decided to become an architect, and he later went to work for J.L. Silsbee in his architectural practice.

There he met someone who was to teach him as much about life as architecture. His name was Cecil Corwin and the two were to remain friends for the next nine years.

Wright had received many prestigious jobs in Chicago and as far east as Buffalo. But it was the Unity Temple that confirmed his position at the top of his profession. It comprised everything

that he had learned so far and extended far beyond, amazing even advanced designers, engineers and contractors in Germany, who had been experimenting with poured-in-place concrete for several years but had yet to attain this level of sophistication.

Wright's choice of concrete was based on sound economics as it was a less expensive material than

ALBERT D. GERMAN WAREHOUSE, RICHLAND CENTER, WISCONSIN, 1915
It is thought that the warehouse was built just south of what may be Frank Lloyd Wright's possible birth place.

The building utilizes an innovative structural system which is sophisticated in the integration of the concrete slabs and flared column capitals, which are ornamented in typical Wright
fashion using the same pre-moulded system as the Unity Temple columns of several years earlier. The exterior top storey is composed of simple brick panels topped with an elaborate concrete section of patterned blocks, which are much finer than those of Midway Gardens. Many think they can detect a Mayan influence, though Wright would possibly not have agreed with them.

either stone or brick. His design was simplicity itself, with plain walls and decorative elements limited to easily reproducible column capitals. Even glazed areas were restrained, being mostly of clear glass crossed with straight lines and no decoration in the clerestory windows. There were no stained-glass windows or rose window above or opposite the altar.

The building included structural, mechanical, electrical and 'visual' systems.

There was an unusual coffered ceiling of 25 squares with rare brown and caramel glass, earth tones which were to appear in later work. This consisted of a three-dimensional slab supported by columns on each of four sides with four hollow columns at the corners that contained the air ducts. In the space below the second tier of seating was a bank of radiators that warmed the concrete and also the air ducted past them. The balconies around three sides reduced the need for floor space and brought the congregation into closer proximity to the minister, providing the congregation with a clear view of the proceedings and producing a feeling of friendly

IMPERIAL HOTEL, TOKYO, JAPAN, 1914–1922

Tokyo's Imperial Hotel was demolished in 1968 and elements of it were reconstructed in this park near Nagoya, many years later.

This was the most important commission of the second stage of Wright's career and placed him firmly as a world-class architect.

There are few colour photographs, but many black-and-white images of the original are available. The brick was a beautiful golden colour with a heavily textured pattern. The roof had clay tiles, in size and colour similar to many that could be seen throughout Tokyo.

The pond was an important

feature in several respects; it produced a beautiful reflection of the entrance with its lily pads and koi carp, and had a cooling effect in the hot Tokyo summers, producing a welcome ambience for arriving guests. On the practical side, it was able to take the water run-off during rainstorms and act as a reservoir in the event of fire or other emergency.

28

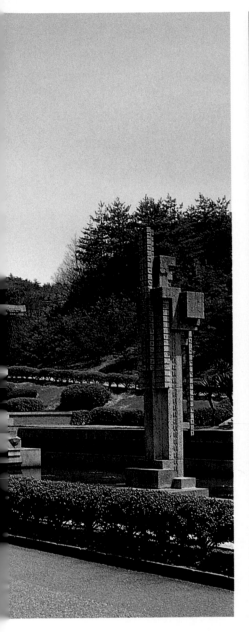

association with one's neighbours.

The need for a new church had arisen because of a fire which had occurred in early June 1905. The new site was donated by an Oak Park real-estate broker, Edwin Gale, and the committee was chaired by a Wright client, Charles E. Roberts, a major industrialist and owner of the Chicago Screw Company.

The building was composed of two major spaces, the temple area and the social room. The entry to the building and the connecting hall between the rooms had the pastor's offices above. The building did not have a particularly religious atmosphere to it; it had no steeple or pitched roof that pointed toward heaven and the Almighty. There

were no bells and no belltower, neither were there crucifixes as in most other Christian churches. Yet there existed what Wright would describe as 'repose', a quality of tranquillity which emanated from the simplicity of the design. Here, the combination of scale and detail creates an unexpected but strangely familiar arrangement that is both

TALIESIN III, SPRING GREEN, WISCONSIN, ILLINOIS, 1925–59

The ultimate evolution of the 1911 Taliesin I, which was damaged by fire in 1914 and again in 1925. Taliesin was a constant source of experimentation for Wright in terms of design. Even though it was always Wright's true home, it was also a workplace for his apprentices.

appropriate and pleasing.

One of the few buildings that did not require a strong protagonist to carry the project through was the Pettit Chapel of 1906, which was designed as a memorial to an

important physician and husband of the client. The chapel was built for the benefit of the entire community where the family had its roots. It was built in a cemetery adjacent to the family grave site rather than in a public thoroughfare. While funeral services have long been the major function, the first wedding was recently held in the chapel.

It was envisaged to be small, even for a house. The one-story stucco chapel has a single room for services with a continuous band of windows on three sides below the hipped roof, as well as a large roofed porch with three sets of

stairs leading down to the grass. The porch was arranged crossways to the room. A basement of sorts, accessed through one of the piers, led to a rest room, situated partially below grade.

The windows have a simple, small-scale pattern of squares and rectangles that impart a quality of luminescence to the walls and enliven the shadows cast by the deep overhang of the roof.

Daily public tours make the Rookery Building one of the most visited of Wright's designs, and tourists are only a small proportion of people visiting the interior daily.

JONES VALLEY, WISCONSIN, ILLINOIS
In 1846, the large extended family of Frank's mother, Anna Lloyd Jones, originally emigrants from Wales, purchased two 40-acre (16-hectare) parcels of land from the government and continued to buy land until they had accumulated about 18,000 acres in all, which the family farmed and where they built their farmhouses (seven in all) and practised self-sufficiency.

This is a view from a guest room at Taliesin, which Frank Lloyd Wright built for himself, and which affords a nearly complete view of the entire Jones Valley. Wright dammed the small stream, creating the lakes and adding many trees that were positioned with the assistance of the famous landscape architect, Jens Jensen.

The third Taliesin of 1925 became Wright's operational headquarters for the rest of his life, even when Taliesin West had made its appearance, and was greatly expanded in all directions to include drafting studios, a music room and extensive gardens for the enjoyment of his family and apprentices.

ARIZONA BILTMORE HOTEL, PHOENIX, ARIZONA, 1928 (LEFT)

Since its original construction, just before the Wall Street Crash of 1929, there have been many additions and alterations, most of them changes made by the firm which succeeded Wright, Taliesin Associated Architects, still working from Taliesin West. These additions include a conference centre and the wings to the east.

These additions presented some interesting problems with innovative solutions: would it have been economical to use the same construction system as was originally used? Yes, and no are the answers. However, in one of the wings, precast concrete panels patterned to seem like the individual blocks of the original have been used, while TAA has tried several other economical solutions.

NATIONAL LIFE INSURANCE COMPANY, CHICAGO, ILLINOIS, 1924 (RIGHT)

Had this 30-storey building been realized, it is possible that Wright's career would have taken a very different direction. The design makes for an efficient and modern skyscraper which was to have had alternating copper and glass panels. The copper was to have been treated with a wash to encourage the development of verdigris, in much the same manner as the Price Tower of the 1950s.

To overcome the lighting problem, the building was planned with four projections to the south, allowing light to be admitted across the entire floors of the offices.

There were four sets of elevators,

one servicing each of the projections and thus distributing the load that occurs at the beginning and end of each working day. Using diagrams, Wright plotted the potential evacuation of the building on a minute-by-minute basis, demonstrating the method by which an even flow could be achieved.

The client was already known to Wright because Edward Waller had commissioned Wright to remodel his personal residence in River Forest several years earlier. The Rookery remodelling of 1906 was to the entrances, court staircase and balcony of a grand design by Daniel Burnham, the original

architect of what was one of Chicago's most famous landmarks.

While Wright's remodelling was more modern than that of the original construction of about 20 years earlier, it was atypical of his work of the time when his Prairie style was in full swing; little of this can be seen in the lobby – carved and gilded marble adorned with curlicues were not typical of Wright's work. There were also stylized, marble flower urns set atop the newel posts at the bottom of the grand staircase, which was a recurring feature of Wright's work.

Waller and Wright's first client, William Winslow, were two of the

founders of the Luxfer Prism Company and had invented a method of waterproofing a stained-glass assembly which utilized prismatic 4-inch (10-cm) square tiles that were intended to direct daylight further into a building. These tiles were used on the alley sides of the Rookery Building as well as on the floor of the lobby walkway and allowed considerably more light to permeate the walkway and filter into the storefronts below. Sadly, the lobby and building were almost lost due to a national economic downturn, but were rescued and restored several years ago.

One of the most successful architectural commissions to have the shortest existence for a building intended to be permanent, Midway Gardens had lasted for less than 10 years when it was demolished in 1923. It appears to have been conceived on a grand scale, when one examines the remaining photographs, and occupied most of a city block in Chicago.

It was to have been a grand beer garden in the European tradition, but while both Europe and Chicago have temperate climates, Chicago's is actually a little more extreme then Paris or London. The hot Chicago summers

OCOTILLO CAMP, NEAR CHANDLER, ARIZONA, 1927 (ABOVE)
The camp was erected for Wright and his assistants to use while designing and developing the site of San-Marcos-in-the-Desert for Alexander Chandler. Wright worked closely within the unfamiliar environment, using materials which had never been considered before.

JOHNSON WAX ADMINISTRATION BUILDING RESEARCH TOWER, RACINE, WISCONSIN, 1944 (RIGHT)
The Research Tower, for large experiments, was added at a later date to the original Johnson Wax Administration Building (overleaf).

JOHNSON WAX ADMINISTRATION BUILDING, RACINE, WISCONSIN, 1936
(AERIAL VIEW)

The entrance to the offices is at the centre of the structure, approached by driving or walking under the bridges behind the great workroom that is closest to the street. At each side of this central entrance are two nostrils that contain the air intake and exhaust mechanisms, plus the elevators and their equipment.

This modern building was located next to the more mundane manufacturing and shipping establishments constructed from concrete frames with infills of brick and clay tile, and is in much the same context as the Larkin company's, located in Buffalo and built nearly 35 years earlier.

The tall research tower (see previous page) was designed and built several years after the main structure. A courtyard was created around the base of the tower which was defined by a low series of offices and also added considerably to the security for the important work going on within the tower's laboratories.

were not nearly as difficult to contend with as the bitter winters that prevented entertainments from being held outside. This made the finances for a largely outdoor venue difficult to balance. The grand opening was held in June 1914 but the project was bankrupt within a few years.

The building itself was similar in its operation to several other European-style beer gardens, both inside and out. Wright resisted the

JOHNSON WAX ADMINISTRATION BUILDING, RACINE, WISCONSIN, 1936

It may not be immediately apparent that there are no doors or windows on the street side, which would have allowed the observer to have some idea of the size of the building. Moreover, it may not be immediately understood that there are bands of glass tubing which have the function of windows.

The corners of the building come in three types, square, rounded, and both square and rounded above. The building does not conform well to any specific description as there are so many exceptions to what one might consider the rule. The building sits solidly on the ground and yet there is an all-glass, tubular bridge connecting two parts of the offices.

Johnson Wax was considered to be a modern-style building at the time of its completion in the late 1930s, as were those built about the same time and commonly called Art Deco. Today, over 60 years later, the Johnson Wax Building maintains its modern appearance, and does not look as dated as many of its contemporaries.

urge to decorate the walls with hanging vines and bunches of grapes and substituted simplified male and female sculptures, some standing alone while others were integrated into light poles – poles with open cubes with light bulbs placed within.

The rough brick building had a stage situated opposite the street, and covered by a canopy that also acted as an acoustical diffuser. Sets

TALIESIN WEST, SCOTTSDALE, ARIZONA, 1938

Wright followed his own advice and went far away from the populated areas to buy a large parcel of land measuring about a square mile (2.6km²). This was at the base of a mountain in an area that had been populated by Native Americans who had left their mark on the landscape, one of them a large boulder covered with enigmatic symbols. Wright placed this in a prominent position at the top of the entry stairs to the drafting room.

of tables and chairs filled the central patio that was surrounded by elevated private boxes for special guests. Towards the street was an enclosed restaurant and dance floor that was described as the Winter Garden. At opposite ends of the entry were wonderful geometrical painted murals, hand-painted by the second son of the architect, John Lloyd Wright.

The National Symphony Orchestra under the conductor Max Bender opened the Gardens with great aplomb and there was a bevy of talented guests, including Russian ballerina Anna Pavlova. Midway Gardens was well on the way to becoming one of the major locations for the very best in entertainment and had wonderful acoustics. Then it was bankrupted, Midway was sold, and its intended purpose underwent a change. There was less music and several hard winters put a financial strain on the second owners. Then the beginning of Prohibition sealed its

Taliesin West, Scottsdale, Arizona, 1938

The living room was predominantly the Wrights' domain. However, on special occasions, it was opened to the entire Fellowship and their guests. On Saturday nights it was also the place for cocktails and conversation before a wonderful dinner was served, with Olgivanna greeting every person present and charming them with the warmth of her personality. The space has changed since the time that its walls were open to the rough desert, and is now air-conditioned.

fate and scheduled the demolition of these remarkable buildings.

It was during the construction of this building, while Wright was on site supervising the construction, that he was notified of the tragedy at Taliesin, where Mamah Cheney, her children and several of Wright's assistants had been brutally attacked and murdered.

Japan had become open to Western trade in 1854 when a Treaty of Peace and Amity was signed between the United States and the Empire of Japan; but it was not until 1867 that such innovations as Western food made an appearance there. A year later marked the beginning of the reign of Emperor Meiji Tenno, the modernizer, and the first Imperial Hotel was opened in 1890. This was planned according to the best Beaux Arts traditions and included Mansard roofs, but it had a wooden frame and was designed by a young Japanese architect.

Unfortunately, an earthquake on 21 June 1894 caused not only considerable damage to the hotel but also to other buildings in Tokyo, as well as equipment that was intended to measure such an event. By 1909, with the increase in visitors to the city, there was pressure to build a much larger and more modern building, increasing capacity to 60 rooms; by 1920 it was able to accommodate 300 guests.

It is not entirely clear how Wright came to be given this commission, and it may be that two sets of rough designs were made before 1914; eventually, the contract was signed on 17 March 1916, in which five percent of the cost of the new construction was made available

At 8.30pm, two days after Christmas 1919, a large fire broke out in room 120 of the 1906 annexe which soon spread, fanned by the strong southwesterly winds, making the construction of the new Wright design even more urgent. Wright was able to secure the services of a construction engineer, Paul Mueller, who had been connected with Adler & Sullivan's office in the 1880s and '90s. Moreover, Mueller had also built Unity Temple and Midway Gardens to Wright's design.

The H-plan and the double-loaded corridors are two features that one might find in any low-rise modern hotel. What was unexpected was the scale, the level of detail, and the use of light, which was probably the most outstanding feature of this glorious building. Tokyo has a beautiful quality of light, much like that of

another city on the Pacific Ocean with a beautiful bay, San Francisco.

The perforated overhang of the low-slung roof and the thin vertical windows contributed to the manipulation of the light as it entered the rooms. The windows were deep-set and the light reflecting off the golden brick jambs warmed the guest rooms during the cold, grey winters. These kept out the noise of one of the largest cities in the world, the thick brick and Oya stone walls

preventing the noise from reverberating through the building and disturbing the guests.

The most surprising feature is the size of the major interior spaces. One enters through a set of low doors and up some stairs to where the ceiling rises, taking in an additional three storeys.

The scale of the custom-designed furniture for the Imperial Hotel suggests a much larger building, perhaps related to the culture and small stature of the

TALIESIN WEST, SCOTTSDALE, ARIZONA, 1938
The ancient petroglyph, found on the site and relocated to this position, sits on the patio leading from the drafting room and overlooking the pool.

TALIESIN WEST, SCOTTSDALE, ARIZONA, 1938

Taliesin West was designed to be a self-contained world of its own, with every facility provided for work and play, including this small theatre.

Japanese people, even though it was to be a hotel for Western visitors.

The hotel was quite large for its time, having 150 guest rooms with baths and telephones, a main banqueting hall and a dining room that could accommodate 1,000, five other ballrooms, ten other banqueting rooms, and an indoor swimming pool, post office and other facilities.

However, the hotel eventually opened without Wright's presence;

he had left Japan on 22 July 1922, never to return. He never saw the completed building.

That Wright had been absent for the planned opening was perhaps fortunate for him. At two minutes to noon on 1 September 1923, the Great Kanto Earthquake hit in the vicinity of Yokohama, about 30 miles (48km) from Tokyo. Tokyo burned for three days before the fire could be controlled. Three quarters of the houses was destroyed and 1.5 million people were made homeless. However, it was only necessary to close temporarily 3 per cent of the rooms in the Imperial Hotel for repairs. There were some cracks and damage to a few columns, otherwise the hotel remained unharmed, making it a refuge in a city full of chaos.

If nature had been unable to destroy the building, economics managed to complete the job. The hotel was demolished in 1968 and replaced by a much taller 17-storey structure. Parts of the original were transported to a park near Nagoya and were reconstructed there along with many other buildings of the Meiji era. One hopes that they will survive for many years.

A growing company in a small town acquires space by purchasing adjacent buildings and moving services into them. When these companies are in a residential neighbourhood, however, perhaps in a University complex, it often means that the offices are situated in houses surrounding the site. This was certainly true of the Johnson Wax company in the 1930s. At first, a conservative approach was contemplated which included remodelling or expanding the existing office space.

Herbert Johnson, the grandson of the founder and president at the time, felt that it was important to provide the best facilities for his employees, and with this in mind he employed a local Racine architect who could be trusted to provide an American image for the company. The new design was a limestone Beaux Arts composition

FLORIDA SOUTHERN COLLEGE (ANN PFEIFFER CHAPEL), LAKELAND, FLORIDA, 1940

Wright was commissioned to plan the campus for a previously unremarkable Methodist college dating from the middle of the 19th century, which turned out to be as remarkable an achievement as the Imperial Hotel of 20 years earlier.

In imitation of Wright, the principal thought it would be good for his students to involve themselves in the construction, but the idea proved inefficient and expensive.

The Pfeiffer Chapel was but one of Wright's fine buildings, sponsored by a benefactor, to appear on the campus.

with indirect lighting through skylights and a new innovation that was finding a wider acceptance, air conditioning. Before this, if the temperature rose above 90 degrees, the employees would have been told to go home.

Johnson and other executives of the company felt that the design was uninspired and in various discussions, Wright's name came up. Johnson met Wright and came away fired with enthusiasm, convinced that Wright would be able to produce exactly what was required.

Wright was already working on a commission from Edgar Kaufmann to design Fallingwater, a large country house, a project which was not, however, sufficient to continue financing the Taliesin Fellowship. Johnson was an intelligent man, willing to take risks, which was just what Wright

needed at the time. Johnson was also able to appreciate the kudos such an innovative design was likely to attract and felt that the expense and frustration involved in such a project would be well worth it in the long run.

A similar approach was adopted for Johnson Wax as that of the Larkin project, but Johnson's idea was to keep the workers' attention focused on their work rather than their environment. Skylights were used effectively to illuminate the working space and there was rubber flooring to eliminate noise and show off to advantage the company's main product – floor wax.

FLORIDA SOUTHERN COLLEGE, LAKELAND, FLORIDA, 1940 (ABOVE AND RIGHT)
The various buildings were designed to be connected by a series of covered walks or esplanades to give shelter in the Florida heat; in total they ran for about 1¹/₂ miles (2.4km). Outside of the connecting esplanades there were ten structures, which included seminar buildings, named for various benefactors, and a water dome. Unfortunately the Second World War intervened, which halted construction, but it was continued in 1954 with the Danforth Chapel. The last building was constructed in 1958.

FRANK LLOYD WRIGHT AT THE GUGGENHEIM, 1956 (ABOVE)

Wright spent many years planning and preparing for the construction of the Guggenheim Museum. Here he is directing the concrete contractor on possible shoring options during the work of construction. He unfortunately died a few months before the museum's completion, but his wife was able to attend the opening ceremony.

Johnson Wax turns itself to the inside, focusing the workers' attention to their desks rather than to the shape of a cloud outside. The building is 245ft (75m) east to west and each of the internal mushroom columns have nearly 29ft (9m) between them.

The building was constructed essentially as Wright initially conceived it in his first sketches. It is of red brick and the windows are composed of glass Pyrex tubes wired to metal frames.

It is as unique and beautiful as

THE SOLOMAN R. GUGGENHEIM MUSEUM, NEW YORK CITY, 1943–59 (RIGHT)

Had the two principals in the development of the Guggenheim Museum not had the fortitude to persevere with this project we would have been deprived of one of the greatest works of architecture ever produced. Wright was first presented with the challenge during the war and the building is all the better for its long gestation; in fact, Wright's creations were usually completed in his head before pen touched paper.

ART CENTER COLLEGE OF DESIGN LIBRARY

the Larkin building, with manipulation of light the most important factor.

However, construction did not proceed smoothly: the design failed to meet building codes and the state Industrial Commission refused to approve the plans and specifications. This did not halt the proceedings entirely but it did necessitate the construction of a full-scale mushroom column so that it could be tested to destruction. Each of the columns was designed to support a maximum of 5 tons, but in the event managed to hold

60 tons before collapsing – many times more than the maximum required to support the building. Wright won the day and construction commenced in earnest.

Wright had designed a building that looked as if it were moving down the street, as sleek as the autos and trains that were regarded as modern in the 1930s. The interior, clad in American walnut, was so unusual that standard office furniture looked completely out of place, so Wright was pleased to design this as well, which turned out to be equally unusual. It was

THE SOLOMAN R. GUGGENHEIM MUSEUM, NEW YORK CITY, 1943–59
The construction of this ambitious project did not always run smoothly and it was probably a source of tribulation for the architect at the end of his long life. The controversial design, as well as the wisdom of using a spiral ramp to display art, was frequently challenged; but is now regarded as a master work that is totally in sympathy with the materials used.

The building is surmounted by a cupola (opposite), a source of illumination in an elegant structure.

constructed from hollow metal tubes, straight or bent into arcs. The desk tops were walnut; the chairs for the general office were three-legged with circular seats and backs that pivoted for comfort. Drawers pivoted and swung out rather than having to be pulled out. Not even the waste paper baskets escaped Wright's notice.

Johnson liked the building so much he returned to Wright for the design of an additional research facility. Wright's answer was a tall tower, with every other floor held inside the walls, which facilitated

large experiments that needed more space than usual. It was constructed much like a tree, with cantilevered floors extending from the main trunk like branches. The windows were given the same glass tubing as the main building and diffused the light in a similar way.

Ill-health was Wright's reason for building Taliesin West in 1938. He had been familiar with the area through his work on the Arizona Biltmore Hotel, and also the San Marcos project for Dr Chandler, which was halted before it was to begin; both of these were in the

1920s. Wright had had pneumonia and his physician advised him, although he was now in his seventies, that if he wished to live a long life, the cold and damp of Wisconsin winters were best avoided. Wright had already experienced the dry and warmer central Arizona winters and focused his search in that area, as yet little developed but with good transportation; land there was also inexpensive.

Wright had founded the Taliesin Fellowship several years earlier with a view to bringing on young

UNITARIAN MEETING HOUSE, SHOREWOOD HILLS, WISCONSIN, 1947

Marshall Erdman, who was later to commission a series of prefabricated houses from Wright, had been an architectural graduate of the University of Illinois at Urbana, and was responsible for the construction of the meeting house.

It sits on a foundation of 9in (23cm) of gravel rather than a concrete footing and wall. The large roof is constructed of large trusses made from very small components covered with a standing seam copper cladding.

The stone walls are the same type of limestone that forms the base of Taliesin, located about 35 miles (56km) to the west.

Wright maintained that the design was based on hands folded in prayer and pointing to heaven.

apprentices, educating them in his methods and eventually utilizing their talents. Wright established an annual trip for them all, transporting them from Wisconsin to Arizona each autumn and returning in the spring. Here they set up camp which every year was expanded and improved and where Wright developed his architectural ideas away from the eyes of clients.

The extreme contrast of the landscape also formed the perfect background to Wright's organic concepts of architecture which he intended to transmit to his students. He also liked to pose problems and encourage his pupils to think for themselves; the act of creating the camp themselves presented opportunities to work out many of the possible solutions to the problems that would inevitably arise. It also invigorated Wright,

V. C. MORRIS GIFT SHOP, SAN FRANCISCO, CALIFORNIA, 1948

Maiden Lane, where the Morris gift shop is situated, is the name of the street, or more properly the alley, that was once the red light district, and is adjacent to the famous Union Square in central San Francisco.

What at first appears to be a very plain façade without windows (opposite), reminiscent of Richardsonian Romanesque, in fact conceals unusual interior details; the descending ramp was already a

preoccupation and was probably the prototype of the Guggenheim Museum which Wright had already conceived but which had not yet been built. There is subtle concealed lighting which allows the goods to be dramatically highlighted without damaging them. Below the horizontal beltline are squares that are also backlit and that lead one into the arched entrance. Within this, a plastered ceiling makes up half of the arch, with glass forming the other half. The gate is a recent addition.

who lived for another 20 years after that first winter spent in Arizona.

The Guggenheim Museum has always been much-discussed, not least because it is one of the rare buildings in the Wright oeuvre that was executed in a circular form. The story of the struggles and triumphs that were endured so that this magnificent structure could exist is compelling. Unfortunately, Frank Lloyd Wright did not live long enough to see it completed; he died just months before it was opened to the public.

PRICE TOWER, BARTLESVILLE, OKLAHOMA, 1952

Harold Price was somewhat startled to find he was to have a skyscraper rather than the low-rise building he had expected. Wright's design, in fact, originated from a plan for St. Mark's-in-the-Bouwerie in New York, which was never realized, and is a combination of residential and office accommodation.

The major four corners of the building are set to the compass points with three-quarters of each floor composed of office space. There are four small elevators that run up and down the central core of the tower, three for the offices and one for the residences. On each floor, between the elevators, is a small lobby and with three elevators in attendance, waiting time was kept to the minimum.

The residential units have dramatic two-storey living rooms, overlooked by two bedrooms.

As with many of Wright's creations there were elements of the unique and unusual guaranteed to cause panic in the minds of city planners everywhere, and even after the final design was agreed, it still took several years of negotiation with various city departments before the feasibility of each component and system was agreed; this was after nearly 17 years of refinements and compromises by both client and the architect.

BETH SHOLOM SYNAGOGUE, ELKINS PARK, PENNSYLVANIA, 1954

The plan of the synagogue is a triangle. The roof is in the form of a tripod which, when combined with gravity, is one of the strongest, most stable formations in nature. As a result of the geometrical strength, the materials used to sheath the framework can be very lightweight, which is especially true in this example.

A framework composed of steel sections supports the corrugated, translucent rectangular panels that form the roof's surfaces. Each of the three surfaces is creased at the centre and stiffened by a trapezoidal diaphragm that laps the crease. The panel section just above the concrete base is set at right angles to the roof plane and lends a distance between ground and the roof plane that makes the building appear much taller than it actually is. There are doors on only one of the faces that give any clue as to the scale of the finished product.

The surface and edges are highly textured with sharp geometric forms, which add to the crystalline effect.

The translucence of the roof allows light to softly permeate the building, while the exterior at night is a dramatic glowing landmark.

The building was meant to suggest Mount Sinai, where God gave the Ten Commandments to Moses. Throughout the building, both inside and out, are many allusions to the history and iconography of the Jewish faith, which Wright had previously discussed with the rabbi.

The design itself is an enormous departure from the traditional museum layout, most of which consist of large rooms with high walls and specialist lighting. Some of them take advantage of the size and include three-dimensional objects toward the centre of the rooms; otherwise, the flat art is hung on the walls in various arrangements. This dull description is certainly true of the vast majority of public art museums still in existence at the beginning of the 21st century.

One of Wright's objectives was to display a mixture of flat and three-dimensional art, all non-objective or abstract art which had been collected by Solomon Guggenheim. Why not see art as the artist did when it was being created? Why not place the flat art on easels set into various locations on a wide downward sweep of a ramp? The sculptures would be set in niches to allow viewers to walk around each piece, while to look across the open atrium from above and below would present vistas

impossible in a conventional venue. Spiral slits were envisaged to allow natural light to mingle with that coming from the circular cupola above. Unfortunately, not all of this was to be. The spiral slits were closed over and electric light was introduced to guarantee consistency of illumination.

However, Wright seems to have preferred the fluctuations of colour and intensity provided by natural light, which gave new and different dimensions to the art, bringing it more accutely to life.

The buff colour of the unadorned surfaces also provided a neutral background to the exhibits, as well as a natural foil for the brilliance of the colours.

From the exterior, the building, though solid, appears rather lighter, as it actually starts one level above the street; its curves give it a dynamic not often seen in conventional art museums.

The design had had its beginnings in a hand-written letter from the curator of the Solomon Guggenheim collection in the summer of 1943, when there was little work at Taliesin because of the Second World War. But it took over 17 years for the project to come to fruition. Progress was very slow and Guggenheim wanted to be assured of the costs, which he thought would come down after the war; however, Guggenheim died in 1949 and the project came almost to a halt. But the final drawings and permits were ready by 1952 and construction was under way by 1956: Wright took such personal interest in the construction that he would take up a trowel to explain some of the finer points to the masons.

The idea of a spiral was a reaction to Wright's visits to museums based on the Beaux Arts

FIRST CHRISTIAN CHURCH, PHOENIX, ARIZONA, 1950
This was originally a design for the South-West Christian Seminary for another site, also in Phoenix. The congregation approached Olgivanna Wright in 1966 to ask her permission to start the building, which was not begun until 1973 and the 122-ft (37-m) bell tower in 1978.

DALLAS THEATER CENTER (THE KALITA HUMPHREYS THEATER), DALLAS, TEXAS, 1955

Two actors, Kalita Humphreys and her husband, Joe Burson, were unfortunately killed in a plane crash and it was Kalita's mother who donated $100,000 to the theatre group and requested that a memorial to her daughter be constructed. Wright became involved in the project as one who liked to provide a creative solution for a difficult site and a tight budget and the group was well pleased with the result.

concept. When walking through the linear, symmetrical galleries of these earlier examples, one had to return the same way one had come, looking at the same pieces of art twice when returning to the entry which was also the exit. Wright envisaged a one-way arrangement. His solution was to have the visitors take an elevator to the top level and for them to take a leisurely stroll down a sloped ramp, viewing the art as they descended.

An art museum with few flat surfaces was a radical idea indeed. Many artists and critics strongly

objected, some in writing, complaining how inappropriate the building was for such an important collection. The list included Willem de Kooning, Robert Motherwell and nearly 20 others.

Wright visited the construction of the Guggenheim for the last time in January 1959 and sadly died the following April without seeing the final result.

A Wright client, Harold C. Price, tells the story of how the Price Tower project began after his sons suggested they commission Wright as architect: 'We desired to build a

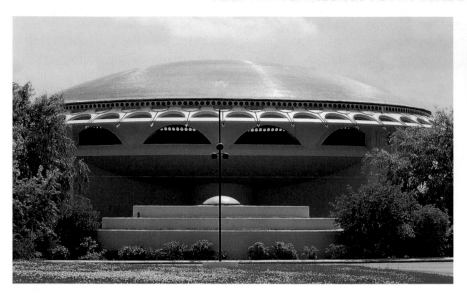

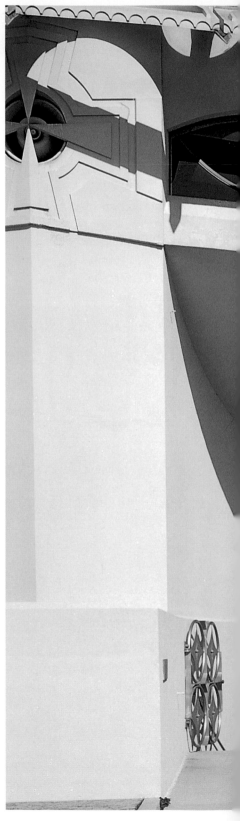

ANNUNCIATION GREEK ORTHODOX CHURCH, WAUWATOSA, WISCONSIN, 1956

Wright's mastery of innovative structural systems has never been properly studied, but this church is an excellent example of a thin-shelled concrete dome.

It was originally covered on the exterior with small 2 x 2-in (5- x 5-cm) dark-blue ceramic tiles which glistened in the sun. The tiles presented a very slippery surface which was able to throw off snow in the winter, which would have otherwise overstressed the dome. The

dome rests on a circle of small steel balls at its edges which act as ball bearings, allowing the dome to move in any direction without cracking.

The design won an award from the Concrete Association for its innovative techniques. The arched windows, now filled with leaded, stained glass, take the stresses admirably and transfer them more effectively than square openings. Just under the roof's edge is a ring of small, round windows filled with plastic domes which allow more light throughout the building.

structure which would be a credit to our city for years to come. However, I did not believe that Mr Wright would be interested in such a small building. My sons telephoned him and made an appointment. We went to Taliesin. I told him I wanted a three-storey building with about 25,000sq ft (2,3225m²) of floor space. He said immediately that three floors was most inefficient and suggested ten

floors of 2,500sq ft (232.25m²) each. We finally compromised on 19 floors, and included apartments with the offices.'

It is said of the tower that, for its time, it was the most expensive office building in the United States. However, Price must have considered it a worthwhile investment, but he could not possibly have envisaged the notoriety it would bring. In the city

ANNUNCIATION GREEK

of Bartlesville, with a population of 19,000, it was the most prominent feature on the horizon, being visible for more than 30 miles (48km).

Wright referred to this design as 'the tree that escaped the crowded forest'. It had originally been proposed in 1929 for a very restricted site in lower Manhattan, New York, called St. Mark's-in-the-Bouwerie, and was to include three towers around a small English-style church. The tree analogy goes further, the central stem of the building being the trunk and the cantilevered floor plates the branches.

The elevators were small and also something of an innovation, being self-service and operated by pushing a button for the desired floor. Before this, all elevators had required an operator on board to answer calls, start and stop the elevator, and open and close the doors. Wright designed cast aluminium furniture that could originally be seen throughout the building.

The sons, Harold, Jr. and Joe Price, were well acquainted with the architect Bruce Goff because they had attended the University of Oklahoma where Goff taught and it was he who suggested they consult Wright concerning the project. Joe Price had had Goff design for him a most unusual house on the family property just east of the house Wright had designed for his father. Joe's house was made of anthracite coal, chunk glass and gold anodized aluminium. Some of the ceilings were covered with white

KENNETH L. MEYERS MEDICAL CLINIC, DAYTONA, OHIO, 1956

The clinic was designed to harmonize with the other buildings in this fine residential neighbourhood. The red brick is very similar to that used in the Johnson Wax building. There is a circular laboratory in the centre of the medical section, with the waiting room set at a 120-degree angle from it.

goose feathers. Apparently, Wright did not completely approve of all this.

Wright had a talent for making something that had never been seen before familiar. However, this is not true of Beth Sholom, conceived in 1954. It is symbolic of Mount Sinai, the location in the Middle East where God gave the Ten Commandments to Moses.

Rabbi Cohen engaged Wright in 1953 because he was confident that Wright would be able to do justice to the design, a 100-foot-high (30-m) mountain of light, and imbue it with an appropriate sense of harmony and grace.

Wright worked to the required image, but the space within looks nothing like a cave within a mountain, and represents the Tent of Meeting that is described in the Book of Exodus, and is flooded with light. The exterior is more akin to a mountain, however, with more than a suggestion of a massed arrangement of jagged rocks. Along the aluminium ridges of the roof are ranged the seven-tiered lamps of the menorahs.

Marin County Civic Center is

THE FRANK LLOYD WRIGHT FOUNDATION VISITORS' CENTER (FORMERLY THE RIVERVIEW TERRACE RESTAURANT), SPRING GREEN, WISCONSIN, 1956
Adjacent to the Taliesin property

and now serving as the visitors' centre for summer tours of the Frank Lloyd Wright Foundation, is the former Riverview Terrace Restaurant, originally commissioned as such by Herbert

Johnson's son-in-law, Willard Keland. However, the building was not completed until after Frank Lloyd Wright's death, when his widow, Olgivanna, involved herself in all the decisions connected with

70

*the decoration of the interior, which
extended not only to fabrics for the
upholstery and colours and finishes
for the walls and floors, but also to
table cloths and napkins, cutlery
and china.*

71

**FASBENDER MEDICAL CLINIC,
HASTINGS, MINNESOTA, 1957**
*As with many of Wright's designs,
the scale of the building is difficult
to determine when looking at it in a
photograph. At first, the roof
appears to be out of proportion to
the size of the structure that it
protects below. A normally-pitched
roof, even with typical Wright-style,
deep overhangs, would still appear
to be too light for the brick walls
holding it up.*

*The copper nearly contacts the
ground and also protects the brick
and mortar joints from the weather.*

*The locations of the windows
are cut through the roof to allow as*

*much sunlight to penetrate to warm
the interior in the cold Minnesotan
winters.*

*The roof resembles a warm
winter cap with its earflaps pulled
down.*

situated on a 160-acre (400-hectare)
site purchased in April 1956. The
County Board of Supervisors
approached Wright in June 1957,
and the plans were pushed through
Wright's office at what some clients
would term 'lightning speed' and
were completed by March 1958.
There were several phases to the
development of the site, added to
the architectural programme a year
after the initial request for Wright's
services.

The site is one that might be
termed typical of the California
landscape: soft, rolling hills covered
with bleached-out grasses. Like the
original plan for the Guggenheim

THE WYOMING VALLEY SCHOOL, SPRING GREEN, WISCONSIN, 1957

This is a small but interesting one-storey school building for a site west of the Jones Valley between two local landmarks, the House-on-the-Rock and Taliesin's Hillside Home School. It was built using standard concrete blocks, but is a far cry from the traditional little one-room schoolhouse.

Museum in New York, one can and must drive under the building to gain access. This is always an unusual feature, but even more so in a Wright building. The building ties the tops of three hills together and pivots at the mid-point.

Arches are good structural devices, not only in earthquake zones such as the San Francisco Bay Area, but also in Europe, where the Romans built many aqueducts. Marin is a poured-in-place concrete construction with a top level of steel, making the upper portions lighter than the lower ones, and better able to resist seismic forces.

On the interior, the offices are set at the outer edges of each floor and there are double corridors, one on each side of an open area at the centre, all lit by skylights above, which are actually clear arch-like structures with metal joints. Corridors and hallways are usually the darkest areas of a building – here they are the lightest.

On the exterior there are corridors or balconies which run around the building, making it unusually simple to access any of the offices.

The first section is asymmetrical, the second wing symmetrical in cross-section. The

MARIN COUNTY CIVIC CENTER, SAN RAFAEL, CALIFORNIA, 1957

Many of Wright's public buildings are rather mysterious and one cannot easily determine what they are all about. The Marin County Civic Center is a case in point: it recalls the familiar aqueducts built by the Romans in Europe, yet the smooth stucco and the blue metallic roof seem so new, even after 50 years, timeless yet grounded in a long tradition.

Again, there are no visible scalar elements such as doors or typical office windows. Wright was able to integrate his buildings so well that it is difficult to determine where the building leaves off and Nature begins. This has as much to do with the construction of the site as the planting and landscaping, introduced after its completion.

two wings meet at the knuckle, a round element that can also be described as a hinge which houses the County Library.

The offices are some of the first to use flexible, re-usable and regularized components. The unit system is an unusual one of 2ft 8in x 5ft 4in (.85 x 1.64m). This is different from most of the houses which are multiples of 2- or 4-ft unit systems.

The parking area was designed to take full advantage of the landscape without dominating it; the lanes are laid out in accordance with natural contours, interspersed by trees and green spaces.

Frank Lloyd Wright approached the design of his public buildings

MARIN COUNTY CIVIC CENTER, SAN RAFAEL, CALIFORNIA, 1957

VIEW OF DOME (LEFT)

The two wings of the building meet at a circular joint, in this case where the County Library is housed below the blue dome. This is important because each wing is composed of different types of rooms and each are of different widths; the circular joint is able to accommodate these differences and the angles formed by the wings.

SIDE ELEVATION (RIGHT)

The office windows are set deep into the stucco arches, which not only adds to the drama of the composition, but also shades the interior to save energy in a state where conservation is one of the foremost concerns. The offices are accessible from interior halls and corridors as well as from walkways created by the inset windows.

in much the same way as his residential work – some of his houses were in fact larger. But it was his humanistic approach that is the main contribution to both. They are scaled to be inhabited by human beings and one always feels a connection with them, when inside or out. One might be impressed by the space or the beauty of the building while never being overwhelmed by its size: the doors, for example, are meant for people and not giants.

Light is perhaps the most important element. It lends character to the spaces and leads one through the buildings by

**GRADY GAMMAGE MEMORIAL
AUDITORIUM, TEMPE, ARIZONA, 1959**
*Wright designed but did not oversee
the construction of the auditorium
which fell to Wes Peters after
Wright's death. The Auditorium's
acoustics are famous for their fine
quality; the grand tier is detached
from the back wall which releases
the sound energy which would
otherwise be trapped under the
balcony.*

means of visual clues. The plans
are logical as one follows the light
to find one's way.

Wright's public buildings are to
be found throughout America and
are still accessible to be enjoyed.
Most have an active tour
programme and welcome visitors
whose number is growing yearly.
Frequent visits will begin to make
one understand the quality of the
design with which Wright was able
to animate them.

Page numbers in italics refer to illustrations